1/5/11

CW01654719

ain

Beyond All Pain

A Companion for the Suffering and Bereaved

A personal selection by

Cicely Saunders

SPCK

First published 1983
SPCK
Holy Trinity Church
Marylebone Road
London NW1 4DU

Selection and arrangement © Cicely Saunders 1983

All rights reserved

British Library Cataloguing in Publication Data

Saunders, Cicely *Dame*
Beyond All Pain
1. Bereavement—Religious aspects—Christianity
I. Title
248.8′6 BV4905.2

ISBN 0-281-04042-7

Filmset, printed and bound in Great Britain by
Hazell Watson & Viney Ltd, Aylesbury, Bucks

Contents

Acknowledgements

Thanks are due to the following for permission to quote from copyright sources:

Constable Publishers for verses from *Lyrics from the Chinese* and *Poetry in the Dark Ages*, translated by Helen Waddell.

James MacGibbon for the poem 'Study to Deserve God' by Stevie Smith, published in *The Collected Poems of Stevie Smith* (Allen Lane).

The Society of the Sacred Cross for the poem 'Fresh Springs'.

BBC Publications for extracts from *Priestland's Progress* (1981) by Gerald Priestland.

Neville Braybrooke (ed.) for an extract from *The Wind and the Rain*, published by Secker and Warburg.

The Faith Press for extracts from *Travels in Oudamovia* by John Austin Baker.

Hodder and Stoughton for extracts from *Man's Search for Meaning* by Victor Frankl.

CRUSE for the poem 'Via Dolorosa' by Margaret Torrie, published in her *Selected Poems*.

The Reform Synagogues of Great Britain for the 'Memorial Service for the Six Million' from *Forms of Prayer for Jewish Worship*.

The publishers have been unable to trace the sources of three anonymous poems. Any information about their origins would be welcomed.

Foreword

Loving inevitably means loss. Death and other devastating disasters cut short what seems to us more important than life itself. Sooner or later we all suffer wounds to make us cry out 'Why should this happen to me?' or, more poignantly '. . . to the one I love?'

Life is learning to love and most of us have merely begun when we die. This is the main reason why many of us long for and expect another life. Even those who have no faith in the promises of religion know that continuity in change is a consistent pattern in this world. Dying followed by a rebirth in a different form happens in many ways; matter and energy are transformed, not destroyed. It would surely be strange if our life of reasoning and loving was the only form of existence to end abruptly, the amazingly subtle energies of our minds the only thing to leave no trace.

The cry of loss may not expect or want an answer but only a silent listening. At other times we are called on to show that we are trying to understand, even though we have few answers to give and no comfort that can take away the pain. But we all have to find some way of handling our own hurts and losses and a means of carrying on in a crippled life. Without this it is difficult to continue to open ourselves to the pain of others or to hold together any belief that there is purpose in life.

This book includes contributions written or dictated

by patients in St Christopher's Hospice who searched for meaning as they faced progressive illness and disability. What they wrote has helped many who knew them and, together with the rest of this personal collection, is offered to others in similar situations and to those who care for them.

1 *The Search for Meaning*

O God, O nameless Someone
That which contains all things yet is not contained,
Be there
What is this in me that cares, that prizes caring above all material things,
But You?
What is this that feels there should be meaning?
Something through and beyond the pain and cruelty
Ravaging this world?
Is it You?
What is this that is so deeply personal?
That longs for that intimate closeness
That yet can be separate?
That seeks to create, to bring out of chaos
An order that is not confined?
That loves beauty and laughter
And that sheer zest of living?
Is it You?

And is it You in the darkness of our minds,
The injustice, the cruelty, the hurricane?
Can it be You in the evil?
Are You buried there?
You Who permeate the universe and beyond,
Gloriously transcendent and yet immediately immanent
Within the minutest particle?
O God, O Nameless Someone,
Be there.

For apart from You, the ground of being
And the transcendent mystery,
There is no meaning.
And cruelty and evil remain,
And pain itself is meaningless.
O God, O Nameless Someone,
Help me to trust;
Not blindly, still walking in uncertainty,
But in trust for the journey
In, through, and out of the desert
O God, O Nameless Someone,
Be there.

P. Thornborough

Down the centuries man has cried out against injustice and suffering.

Written in 780 BC

No man is in the fields,
The forest's stripped and bare,
A few poor faggots left,
And there is none to care.

These men are in great place,
And still they grind the State.
The people cry to heaven,
And think that God is great.
– Is He too great to hate?

translated by Helen Waddell

In the ninth century Alfred the Great translated Boethius, writing in the Dark Ages:

Thou guidest all things to their certain goal
All but the ways of men:
Keep them in check Thou wilt not.
O Ruler of the world, Thou hast spat them out.
Why should the noxious consequence of sin
Take hold upon the sinless?

O Thou, who e'er Thou art,
Thou who dost bind all things in covenant,
Now, now look down on these unhappy lands.
We are not the vilest part of Thy creation,
Great though it be – men tossed on bitter seas.
Rein in the surging of wild rushing waters,
And Thou that rulest heaven's immensity,
By that same covenant, steady the earth.

Translated by Helen Waddell

Memorial Service for the Six Million

We remember our six million dead, who died when madness ruled the world and evil dwelt on earth. We remember those we knew, and those whose very name is lost.

We mourn for all that died with them; their goodness and their wisdom, which could have saved the world and healed so many wounds. We mourn for the genius and the wit that died, the learning and the laughter that were lost. The world has become a poorer place and our hearts become cold as we think of the splendour that might have been.

We stand in gratitude for their example of decency and goodness. They are like candles which shine out from the darkness of those years, and in their light we know what goodness is – and evil.

We salute those men and women who were not Jews, who had the courage to stand outside the mob and suffer with us. They, too, are Your witnesses, a source of hope when we despair.

Because of our people's suffering, may such times never come again, and may their sacrifice not be in vain. In our daily fight against cruelty and prejudice, against tyranny and persecution, their memory gives us strength and leads us on.

In silence we remember those who sanctified His name on earth.

Forms of Prayer for Jewish Worship

Even in the death camps men still searched for a meaning in their lives and in their deaths. Viktor Frankl quotes from Nietzsche 'He who has a *why* to his life can bear with almost any *how*.' He also writes:

> The experiences of camp life show that man does have a choice of action. There were enough examples, often of a heroic nature, which proved that apathy could be overcome, irritability suppressed. Man *can* preserve a vestige of spiritual freedom, of independence of mind, even in such terrible conditions of psychic and physical stress.
>
> We who lived in concentration camps can remember the men who walked through the huts comforting others, giving away their last piece of bread. They may have been few in number, but they offer sufficient proof that everything can be taken from a man but one thing: the last of the human freedoms – to choose one's attitude in any given set of circumstances, to choose one's own way.
>
> Viktor Frankl

For us, as prisoners, these thoughts were not speculations far removed from reality. They were the only thoughts that could be of help to us. They kept us from despair, even when there seemed to be no chance of coming out of it alive. Long ago we had passed the stage of asking what was the meaning of life, a naive query which understands life as the attaining of some aim through the active creation of something of value. For us, the meaning of life embraced the wider cycles of life and death, of suffering and of dying.

Viktor Frankl

Enid's Meditation

Enid fought her way to peace and we often had to battle alongside her. She found her profound dependence hard to bear and could be difficult and demanding. Such struggles towards acceptance are often prolonged, as the same battle is fought over and over again and never seems to be finished. She asked sometimes angry but honest questions of the God she deeply believed in and had served during her active life and after a long battle she gradually accepted the reality of what was happening and found the answer which she has left us, dictated during the month before she died.

A friend and I were considering life and its purpose. I said, even with increasing paralysis and loss of speech, I believed there was a purpose for my life, but I was not sure what it was at that particular time. We agreed to pray about it for a week. I was then sure that my present purpose is simply to receive other people's prayers and kindness and to link together all those who are lovingly concerned about me, many of whom are unknown to one another. After a while my friend said: 'It must be hard to be the wounded Jew when, by nature, you would rather be the Good Samaritan.'

It is hard: it would be unbearable were it not for my belief that the wounded man and the Samaritan are inseparable. It was the helplessness of the one that brought out the best in the other and linked them together.

In reflecting on the parable, I am particularly interested in the fact that we are not told the wounded man recovered. I have always assumed that he did, but now it occurs to me that even if he did not recover, the story will still stand as a perfect example of true neighbourliness. You will remember that the story concludes with the Samaritan asking the innkeeper to take care of the man, but he assures him of his own continuing interest and support: so, the innkeeper becomes linked.

If, as my friend suggested, I am cast in the role of the wounded man, I am not unmindful of the modern day counterparts of the Priest and Levite, but I am overwhelmed by the kindness of so many 'Samaritans'. There are those who, like you, have been praying for me for a long time and constantly reassure me of continued interest and support. There are many others who have come into my life – people I would never have met had I not been in need, who are now being asked to take care of me. I like to think that all of us have been linked together for a purpose which will prove a means of blessing to us all.

Enid Henke

Another patient with paralysis who suffered keenly all the humiliations of loss and dependence found an unexpected freedom and fellowship there and came close to God in the end. He came to the Poetry Workshop where others had to read his poems for him.

Fall

Pride went before
– I fell –
Pride went

James Haylock Eyre

Smoke Rings

I can't blow smoke rings any more:
My tongue, it will not budge,
But other people's various powers
I never would begrudge.

It's not for me to jealous be
And make a silly fuss.
If everybody were like me
Then who'd look after us?

The more I lose my little skills,
The more I see God's plan,
I see what really counts with Him:
The essence of a man.

James Haylock Eyre

Prayer

I find prayer so powerful
That I need but one:
Heavenly Father
Grant me the wisdom
To see the good
In everyone
And everything.
You know my needs:
I do not need to ask.
I appreciate your gifts.
Amen.

James Haylock Eyre

What was really needed was a fundamental change in our attitude towards life. We had to learn ourselves and, further more, we had to teach the despairing men, that it did not really matter what we expected from life, but rather what life expected from us. We needed to stop asking about the meaning of life, and instead to think of ourselves as those who were being questioned by life – daily and hourly. Our answer must consist, not in talk and meditation, but in right action and in right conduct. Life ultimately means taking the responsibility to find the right answer to its problems and to fulfil the tasks which it constantly sets for each individual.

These tasks, and therefore the meaning of life, differ from man to man, and from moment to moment. Thus it is impossible to define the meaning of life in a general way. Questions about the meaning of life can never be answered by sweeping statements. 'Life' does not mean something vague, but something very real and concrete, just as life's tasks are also very real and concrete.

Viktor Frankl

2 *Anger*

What do we do with our anger when we have been hurt? The goal, if we can achieve it, would be to *be angry at the situation*, rather than at ourselves, or at those who might have prevented it or are close to us trying to help us, or at God who let it happen. Getting angry at ourselves makes us depressed.

Being angry at other people scares them away and makes it harder for them to help us. Being angry at God erects a barrier between us and all the sustaining, comforting resources of religion that are there to help us at such times. But being angry at the situation, recognizing it as something rotten, unfair, and totally undeserved, shouting about it, denouncing it, crying over it, permits us to discharge the anger which is a part of being hurt, without making it harder for us to be helped.

Harold Kushner

Not all tears come before the King. Sullen tears, and tears accompanying the petition for vengeance do not ascend on high. But tears of entreaty and penitence, and tears beseeching relief, cleave the very heavens, open the portals and ascend to the King of kings.

Zohar *Forms of Prayer for Jewish Worship*

We do not even know how we are supposed to pray. All we do is call for help because of the need of the moment. But what the soul intends is spiritual need, only we are not able to express what the soul means. That is why we do not merely ask God to hear our call for help, but also beg Him who knows what is hidden, to hear the silent cry of the soul.

Chasidic *Forms of Prayer for Jewish Worship*

What happens is that the quality of depression deepens our sense of unworthiness, our sense of badness and isolation. We interpret this as a distancing from God, instead of a sheer human need that wants God more than ever.

You *never* lose the love of God, you never lose the love of your parents. Temporarily you are out of touch with one another, and guilt is the warning of that. It should do nothing to your basic goodness or to your self-esteem.

The Church has done something that is seriously wrong. It has confused this signal of God's continuous love for us with making a person feel totally bad and unworthy. Nowhere in the Bible is there the message that sin alienates man completely from God. But Christianity has failed abysmally to help people realise that when they feel guilty they do not have to reject themselves totally as bad.

Jack Dominian

The Fourth Word

And at the ninth hour Jesus cried with a loud voice, 'Eloi, Eloi, lama sabachthani?' which means 'My God, my God, why have you forsaken me?'

In this fourth word from the cross Christ went into the lowest depths to which man comes. There he laid himself as a foundation by which we may pass over – like a man laying concrete across a swamp . . . However great the depth of sorrow or shame you or I may be in, it is not bottomless. He went lower still – so that we might pass over.

Bernard Clements

Once he had seen his sin as a thing that clung close as his shadow clung to his heels; now he knew that it was the very stuff of his soul. Never could he, a leaking bucket not to be mended, retain God's saving Grace, however freely outpoured. Never could he, that heavy lump of sin, do any other than sink, and sink again, however often Christ, walking on the waves, should stretch His hand to lift and bring him safe.

He did not know that though the bucket be leaky it matters not at all when it is deep in the deep sea; and the water both without it and within. He did not know, because he was too proud to know that a man must endure to sink and sink again, but always crying upon God, never for shame ceasing to cry, until the day when he shall find himself lifted by the bland swell of that power, inward, secret, as little to be known as to be doubted, the power of omnipotent grace in tranquil, irresistible operation.

H.F.M. Prescott

This prayer and others following come from a book written by four Lithuanian girls imprisoned for their faith in Northern Siberia. Only 2 × 3 inches in size, it was smuggled out of camp with this inscription:

Frances,
We send this prayer book to you in order that you may be able better to feel, think and worship the Lord together with us. Lioné made it, Valé drew it, Leonté glued it together and I wrote it. Ad(elé)

Jesus Falls the Third Time

Depressing despair,
boundless anguish of soul,
crushing fatigue of body,
powerlessness of old age
pinion the wings of soaring spiritual flights.

Prayer

Dead-tired Jesus, help me and my dear ones to endure patiently the helpless weakness of our souls and bodies.

Lithuanian Prisoners

When Christ said 'I was in prison and you visited me,' he did not draw a distinction between the guilty and the innocent.

Pope John Paul II

It is all grace. It is not even that there is a door which Christ has unbolted, and we, standing outside it, have to stretch out our hand, lift the latch, and walk through. We are already inside. When our Saviour became man and undid the sin of Adam, he did not command the cherubim with the flaming sword to return to heaven so that we could re-enter Eden. He picked up the walls of Eden and carried them to the farthest edge of Ocean, and there set them up so that they now girdle the whole world. All we are asked to do is to open our eyes and recognise where we are. Once we have done that, then we shall look down at ourselves and our filthy bodies and our tattered clothes, and we shall say, 'I am not fit to be here, in Paradise'; and we shall ask for baptism to wash us clean, and for the white robe of chrism to clothe us in the righteousness of the Lord. But not in order that we may be saved – simply because this is fitting for those who have been saved.

John Austin Baker

He died that we might be forgiven.
He died to make us good;
That we might go at last to Heaven,
Saved by his precious blood.

This is the shortest and also the most classic statement of the doctrine of the Atonement, but on the question of how His death procures these benedictions and deliverances for us through all the centuries of time, the most elaborate poetry (of which there is but little) takes us no further than the few pregnant lines which Shakespeare gives to Isabella in 'Measure For Measure':

Alas, alas!
Why, all the Souls that were, were forfeit once.
And He that might the vantage best have took
Found out the remedy: how would you be,
If He, which is the top of judgement, should
But judge you as you are? O' think on that,
And mercy then will breathe within your lips,
Like one new made

Roger Lloyd

Love (III)

Love bade me welcome: yet my soul drew back,
 Guiltie of dust and sinne.
But quick-ey'd Love, observing me grow slack
 From my first entrance in,
Drew nearer to me, sweetly questioning,
 If I lack'd any thing.

A guest, I answer'd, worthy to be here:
 Love said, You shall be he.
I the unkinde, ungratefull? Ah my deare,
 I cannot look on thee.
Love took my hand, and smiling did reply,
 Who made the eyes but I?

Truth Lord, but I have marr'd them: let my shame
 Go where it doth deserve.
And know you not, sayes Love, who bore the blame?
 My deare, then I will serve.
You must sit down, sayes Love, and taste my meat:
 So I did sit and eat.

George Herbert

It seems to me that the key to this is that God's *only* power is love-in-the-form-of-grace – not coercion, not the threat of hell-fire, not tinkering with the laws of Nature; and that love is easily rejected. Accepted, it is unconquerable. But the essence of the human condition, as the Christian faith interprets it, is that while we cannot escape God's love (it is offered freely and unconditionally to everyone) we are also free to refuse to respond to it. God, then, is *trying* to be active in every second of history, and in every glimpse and gesture of Nature. But most of the time man frustrates Him. God, maddeningly, refuses to hit back; carries on loving.

Gerald Priestland

Wilt thou not yield me vision,
Lord of grace,
Of that vast realm
Of unhorizoned space
Which is thy heart
That heart-room makes for all?

Alistair Maclean

Even though the day be laden and my task dreary and my strength small, a song keeps singing in my heart. For I know that I am thine.

I am part of thee. Thou art kin to me and all my times are in thy hand.

Alistair Maclean

3 *Suffering*

Over the centuries an all-embracing plan seems in truth to be unfolding around us. Something is afoot in the universe, some issue is at stake, which cannot be better described than as a process of gestation and birth; the birth of the spiritual reality formed by the souls of men and by the matter which they bear along with them. Laboriously, through the medium and by virtue of human activity, the new earth is gathering its forces, emerging and purifying itself. No, we are not like the blooms in a bunch of flowers, but rather the leaves and blossoms of some great tree on which all things appear in due season and due place, in time with and at the behest of the All.

In a bunch of flowers it would be surprising to find imperfect or sickly blooms, because they have been picked one by one and assembled with art. On a tree, by contrast, which has had to fight the internal hazards of its own growth, and the external hazards of rough weather, the broken branches, the bruised blossoms and the shrivelled, sickly or faded flowers are in their rightful place; they reflect the amount of difficulty which the trunk which bears them has undergone before attaining its growth.

The world, looked at empirically on our scale, is an immense groping, an immense search, an immense attack; it can only progress at the cost of many failures and many casualties. The sufferers, whatever the nature of their suffering, are the reflection of this austere but noble condition. They are not useless and diminished elements. They are merely those who pay the price of universal progress and triumph. They are the ones who have fallen on the field of honour.

Teilhard de Chardin

Do not make the mistake
of imagining that you
may go singing
on the Via Dolorosa;
neither may you
bear right or left –
the way is confined
with little room
for manoeuvre.

You will know exhaustion
kneeling often;
trodden and rough
and scarred by many feet
this way is our way
and may not be shunned,
turned from
or avoided –
best to go quietly
with dogged courage
knowing that
one thing is certain –
There is an end.

And when you arrive
you will find
that the hill is crowned
with a living tree
stretching out
great branches
to give you shelter
and manna there
and spring water

Margaret Torrie

I do not beg You to reveal to me the secret of Your ways – I could not bear it. But show me one thing; show it to me more clearly and more deeply: show me what this, which is happening at this very moment, means to me, what it demands of me, what You, Lord of the world, are telling me by way of it. Ah, it is not why I suffer, that I wish to know, but only whether I suffer for Your sake.

Levi Yitzchak of Berditchev
Forms of Prayer for Jewish Worship

Offering

O Lord, because of Your greatest love,
You descended from heaven and walked
the paths of this earth doing good.
You have endured most painful sufferings
in soul and in body.
You have chosen me
to walk the road of the elect.
I wish to follow You, O Lord,
only lead me, give me
strength and wisdom,
and brighten my desires.
With a grateful heart,
I shall accept all from Your hands:
powerlessness, endless longing,
contempt, neglect and disregard,
the loss of those dearest to me
and of my liberty.
Lord, do with me
whatever You desire;
only have compassion on my nation
and on my beloved ones.

Lithuanian Prisoners

Holy Communion

When my soul sheds its tears,
when my heart languishes in longing,
when my whole being shivers in fatigue,
come, O Jesus, I beg You to come.
Draw near, Reviver and Consoler!
What is it You wish to tell me
by means of these people,
by these circumstances,
by this span of time?
Jesus, I implore You to shorten
the time of trial for us
for my dear ones, for my exhausted nation.
Jesus, I ask You – help those
who laid down their lives for our welfare;
assist them for whom You wish me to pray.

Lithuanian Prisoners

For the Hallowing of Suffering

O Lord we pray thee for all weighed down with the mystery of suffering. Reveal thyself to them as the God of love who thyself doest bear all sufferings. Grant that they may know that suffering borne in fellowship with thee is not waste or frustration, but can be turned to goodness and blessing greater than if they had never suffered, through him who on the cross suffered rejection and hatred, loneliness and despair, agonizing pain and physical death, and rose victorious from the dead, conquering and to conquer, even Jesus Christ, our Lord.

George Appleton

What a vast ocean of human suffering is represented by the whole of the suffering on earth at any moment! But what makes up that mass? Blackness, deficiency, waste? No, we repeat, but rather potential energy. In suffering is concealed, with extreme intensity, the world's power of ascension. The whole problem is to liberate it by making it conscious of what it means and what it can achieve. What a leap forward the world would make towards God if all sick people at the same time converted their pain into a common desire that the reign of God should rapidly mature through the conquest and organization of the earth.

The Cross is the symbol and the focus of an action whose intensity is inexpressible. Even from an earthly point of view, fully understood, Jesus crucified is not outcast or defeated. He is, on the contrary, the one who bears the weight and bears always higher towards God the progress of the universal advance. Let us do likewise, that we may be united with him all the days of our life.

Teilhard de Chardin

For the Sick in Mind

O Holy Spirit who dost delve into all things, even the deep things of God and the deep things of man, we pray thee to penetrate the springs of personality of all who are sick in mind, to bring them cleansing, healing and unity. Sanctify all memory, dispel all fear, bring them to love thee with all their mind and will, that they may be made whole and glorify thee for ever.

George Appleton

A Sufficient Prayer

Lord, he whom thou lovest is sick. Do for him according to his need, dear Lord.

George Appleton

There is only one way in which, with the world as it is, God can show himself good in respect of man's suffering; and that is by not asking of us anything that he is not prepared to endure himself. He must share the dirt and the sweat, the bafflement and loneliness, the pain, the weakness, yes, and the death too. That would be a God one could respect, a God who put aside all his magic weapons, and did it all as one of us. A God who, when we cry out in our misery (as we all do), 'Why should this happen to me?' can answer truthfully, 'It happened to me too, not because I couldn't help it happening, but because I chose that it should, because it was right'. Then and then alone will our doubts be stilled, not because we understand, but because we can trust.

John Austin Baker

As he crashes, the airman meets Christ and sees the pattern of salvation.

AIRMAN (at the foot of the steps)

Sir, I understand now what I ought to do.
Am I too late to bring to the wood of Your Cross
Whatever in me is guilty and ought to be crucified?
Whatever, being innocent, is privileged to die in
  Your Death?

PERSONA DEI

The moment when you meet Me is never too late,
Though the moment of death and moment of
  choice were one.
Take up the Cross and come and follow Me,
For you shall carry the burden of bewilderment:
We shall find one another in the darkest hour of
  all.

Dorothy L. Sayers

I, if I be lifted up from the earth, will draw all men to me.

John 12.32

If I can now forgive, it is only because I have been forgiven, I and all the other men and women who have ever lived. Certainly one can forgive only what has been done to oneself. But all the evil ever done has been done to God, because it is a misuse of his good gifts, a rejection of the purposes he set in motion from the beginning. The crucified Jesus is the only accurate picture of God the world has ever seen, and the hands that hold us in existence are pierced with unimaginable nails. But on this Cross God fulfils the nature of forgiveness by using the evil done to him as the means to a new good; for it is the Cross of Jesus which creates within me a free, unhesitating acceptance of the law of love.

John Austin Baker

Nails would not have held God-and-Man fastened to the Cross, had Love not held Him there.

St Catherine of Siena

Wouldst thou learn thy Lord's meaning in this thing? Learn it well: Love was his meaning. Who showed it thee? Love. What showed He thee? Love. Wherefore showed it He? For Love.

Julian of Norwich

Once, in St Paul's Cathedral, I was listening to the magnificent chanting of the Nicene Creed. The setting reiterated and lingered over that one clause, 'He suffered'. 'He suffered, He suffered . . .' it was as if the singers could not get themselves away from the possessing word. They were but preluding the song of Heaven. The Lord, whom we shall worship, and rejoice in, and serve for ever – He is for ever He who suffered, and suffered so that to have suffered abides in Him in power through all the endless age.

H. C. G. Moule

Ascension Prayer

Jesus, You revealed to us
an infinite secret of the soul:
mercy without limit, all-conquering love,
the power that springs from humility,
suffering, and sorrow;
all this You have manifested
as a healing balm for the soul.
Jesus, led by angels, Seraphim and Cherubim,
You ascended to heaven
for the jubilation of saints.

Lithuanian Prisoners

O Lord God, our heavenly Father, regard we beseech thee, with thy divine pity the pains of all thy children; and grant that the Passion of our Lord and his infinite love may make fruitful for good the tribulations of the innocent, the sufferings of the sick, and the sorrows of the bereaved; through him who suffered in our flesh and died for our sake, the same thy Son our Saviour Jesus Christ.

A prayer of the First World War, France 1915
Scottish Prayer Book 1929

Christmas Venite

Let not my humble presence affront and stumble
your hardened hearts that have not known my
ways
nor seen my tracks converge to this uniqueness.
Mine is the strength of the hills that endure and
crumble,
bleeding slow fertile dust to the valley floor.
I am the fire in the leaf that crisps and falls
and rots into the roots of the rioting trees.
I am the mystery rising, surfacing
out of the seas into these infant eyes
that offer openness only and the unfocusing
search for an answering gaze. O recognize,
I am the undefeated heart of weakness.
Kneel to adore, fall down to pour your praise:
you cannot lie so low as I have been always.

John V. Taylor

'When He was born a man,' she said, 'He put on the leaden shroud that's man's dying body. And on the Cross it bore Him down, sore heavy, dragging against the great nails, muffling God, blinding Him to the blindness of a man. But there, darkened within that shroud of mortal lead, beyond the furthest edge of hope, God had courage to trust yet in hopeless, helpless things, in gentle mercy, holiness, love crucified.

'And that courage, Wat, it was too rare and keen and quick a thing for sullen lead to prison, but instead it broke through, thinning lead, fining it to purest shining glass, to be a lamp for God to burn in.

'So men may have courage, then they will see how bright God shines.'

H. F. M. Prescott

4 *Dying*

Study to Deserve Death

Study to deserve Death, they only may
Who fought well upon their earthly day,
Who never sheathed their swords or ran away.

See, such a man as this now proudly stands,
Pale in the clasp of Death, and to his hands
Yields up the sword, but keeps the laurel bands

Honour and emulate his warrior soul,
For whom the sonorous death-bells toll;
He after journeying has reached his goal.

Prate not to me of suicide,
Faint heart in battle, not for pride
I say Endure, but that such end denied
Makes welcomer yet the death that's to be died.

Stevie Smith

Beautiful Old Age

It ought to be lovely to be old
to be full of the peace that comes of experience
and wrinkled ripe fulfilment.

The wrinkled smile of completeness that follows a life
lived undaunted and unsoured with accepted lies.
If people lived without accepting lies
they would ripen like apples, and be scented like pippins
in their old age.

Soothing, old people should be, like apples
when one is tired of love.
Fragrant like yellowing leaves, and dim with the soft
stillness and satisfaction of autumn.

And a girl should say:
It must be wonderful to live and grow old.
Look at my mother, how rich and still she is! –

D. H. Lawrence

They then addressed themselves to the water, and entering, Christian began to sink, and, crying out to his good friend Hopeful, he said, I sink in deep waters; the billows go over my head, all His waves go over me. Selah.

Then said the other, Be of good cheer, my brother: I feel the bottom, and it is good. Then said Christian, Ah! my friend, the sorrows of death hath compassed me about, I shall not see the land that flows with milk and honey. And with that a great darkness and horror fell upon Christian, so that he could not see before him. Also here he in great measure lost his senses, so that he could neither remember nor orderly talk of any of those sweet refreshments that he had met with in the way of his pilgrimage.

[But Hopeful said], These troubles and distresses that you go through in these waters, are no sign that God hath forsaken you; but are sent to try you, whether you will call to mind that which heretofore you have received of His goodness, and live upon Him in your distresses.

Then I saw in my dream, that Christian was in a muse awhile. To whom also Hopeful added these words, Be of good cheer, Jesus Christ maketh thee whole. And with that Christian brake out with a loud voice, Oh, I see Him again; and He tells me, When thou passest through the waters, I will be with thee; and through the rivers, they shall not overflow thee. Then they both took courage, and the enemy was after that as still as a stone, until they were gone over. Christian therefore presently found ground to stand upon, and so it followed that the rest of the river was but shallow. Thus they got over.

John Bunyan

I think a lot of old people just aren't very sensible. They only have old friends and then they live to be ninety or something, like me, and then they start moaning because their friends have gone before, as they say.

My advice to the aged woman is find some young people. Don't go to these dreadful old folks' clubs but find some young people. Put up with their casualness because it's worth it. *Why*, I should like to know, are they so casual, I wonder?

I don't dread dying in my sleep but I do dread dying any other way. Mostly for the nuisance, you know. And I don't dread being dead. My heavenly Father has looked after me from the cradle and he won't stop at the grave. Through all my life he has taken care of me. Even if I just went out like a candle, what is there to dread?

Clergyman's widow, aged 92

Diminuendo

Age is a long, long weaning from the world.
I should have said that hardly yet had I the loving
of it right.
Why learn to love and turn to go? Why sleep by
day and night?
Now there is too much world to love, and no out
that I know
But love more slow, but choose and go, but sleep
by night and day
And only to unusual joy, rise up, rise up, obey.

Grace Goldin

There need be no twilight. A man has Christ. Is he not the truth?' he whispered. 'Is he not the light? Is he not the keeper of the treasure we seek so blindly?'

An Islesman

We are dying, we are dying, so all we can do
is now to be willing to die and build the ship
of death to carry the soul on the longest journey.

A little ship, with oars and food
and little dishes, and all accoutrements
fitting and ready for the departing soul.

Now launch the small ship, now as the body dies
and life departs, launch out, the fragile soul
in the fragile ship of courage, the ark of faith
with its store of food and little cooking pans
and change of clothes,
upon the flood's black waste
upon the waters of the end.

D. H. Lawrence

After a life of many vicissitudes and some months of pain, Sidney Reeman was found to have cancer of his gullet, already inoperable. During his four months in St Christopher's Hospice he found peace and started writing poetry again after a long gap.

From a series of poems written before his death.

Butterflies

Lord, it would be idle
to pretend that I have no fears;
Even tho' I am full of faith
And I am mindful of thy mercy,
And I am hedged about
By Your almighty assurances,
I still advance towards you
With joy in anticipation
And fear of the uncharted seas,
Although I know not the day
Of your beckoning, my faith tells me
To mark off the days like a homesick
Schoolboy puts pen through the days
Separating him from homecoming,
So I, above all, long for the freedom
Of the sons of God. Lord give me
Inward peace, take away all fear.

Sidney G. Reeman
19 Jan 1975

Pressing Business

As life gathers momentum
And one reaches
The Tattenham Corner of the soul
The galloping hooves are thudding
As one races for the post
Lord, so little time and so much to do
Love urges us on
You have given me peace and happiness
In which to end my days
There is so much to do
Sweeping and cleaning
To make room for You
Such a sense of urgency
To commit thoughts to paper
So little time and so much to do
Lord, urge me on.

Sidney G. Reeman
23 Jan 1975

Income and Expenditure

It costs much
To give ourselves
It costs much more
To be the recipient
This requires humility
No man likes to lose
His measure of independence
Suddenly the ground has given way
From under his feet.
Our resources are like a rivulet
Which has drained dry
And we have to ask for water
But I know I depend on Christ
And so it is to Him I turn
The Fountain of Living Water
I shall not thirst,
I am not too proud
To beg of the Lord,
Thanks be to God.

Sidney G. Reeman
25 Jan 1975

In the Midst of Life

Death and I are only nodding acquaintances
We have not been formally introduced
But many times I have noticed
The final encounter
Here in this hospice,
I can truly say
That death has been met with dignity
Who can divine the thoughts
Of a man in close confrontation?
I can only remember
One particular passing
When a man,
With sustained smile
Pointed out what was for him
Evidently a great light
Who knows what final revelations
Are received in the last hours?
Lord, grant me a star in the East
As well as a smouldering sunset.

Sidney G. Reeman
28 Jan 1975

Murmurings

Low murmurings from your creation, Lord
Despite the fact that I am full of thy praise.
In your supreme wisdom, Lord,
You have endowed me
With something more than I can swallow.
I do not pretend to understand
The pattern of your handiwork
Save that in a mysterious way
It helps me to magnify you.
You have wrought wonders in me, Lord,
No slim volume would suffice
To contain the Litany of your praise.
But perhaps a booklet
For, dare I call them, bones of contention,
For example, in the midst of tribulation
Was it quite necessary, Lord,
To allow my specs to nose-dive
And break on the bathroom floor?

Sidney G. Reeman
3 Feb 1975

Coming up for the Third Time

Lord, in the last six days,
I have felt peculiarly plaintive,
Strength seems to be ebbing away
My tale is a tale of woe
Now in the midst of a melancholy moment
Preoccupation about pain
And thoughts squandered about swallowing
I realise that I am
A man of little faith
And it is certainly true
That if Christ were to beckon me
Across the waves, immediately
I should begin to sink
Through sheer lack of confidence
Lord, confirm me in faith
Each time you come with comfort
As the Bread of Life, then
I shall realise that the Divine Strength
Is not ebbing away,
But gathering in intensity.

Sidney G. Reeman
7 Feb 1975

Heaven

The imagination runs riot
In visualising heaven.
Is heaven really
Like the background music
To a Hollywood biblical epic?
Is heaven a magnified
Hallelujah Chorus
Sung by an augmented
Huddersfield Choir?
We can easily imagine
What heaven is not.
All I need know
This side of the trumpets sounding
Is that heaven
Is the vision of my God
Seeing all things and acting in Him.

Sidney G. Reeman
9 Feb 1975

Lost Property

Priceless is that which I have lost
Priceless because irretrievable.
Two days at least seemed
To have passed me by
In a fortnight of existence
Rather uncanny
To think that yesterday is today
And today is yesterday
But the hospice has given reassurance
As well as sustenance
Has given me twelve large hampers
Duly strained and liquidised
The Bread of Life here below
The Great Supper is awaiting
Ever awaiting.

Sidney G. Reeman
24 Feb 1975

Sidney died in the morning of 1 March 1975.

The mountain tarn empties itself by evaporation; its waters are stolen away by sunbeams; they have not perished, they have given themselves to the sunbeams; and have suffered change, and now in the subtle, impalpable form of mist they can steal up the hot bare crags of the mountain and invade with freshness its most secret glens, and soon, when the air grows cool, will hang jewels upon every gossamer thread and bring life to every fainting leaf and blade of grass. So Christ by His sacrifice for us, by the self-emptying of the Incarnation, acquired a new power of stealing into wounded and sorrowful hearts in their extremest dejection and dryness. He comes by His saving death to dying people . . . The mystery of Christ's love in death can steal into that silence, and fill that supreme emptiness . . . In the hour of death and the day of judgement, Good Lord, deliver us.

Fr. Congreve

You were my death;
You I could hold
when all fell away from me.

Paul Gelan
Forms of Prayer for Jewish Worship

Thou angel of God who hast charge of me,
From the dear Father of mercifulness
The shepherding kind of the folds of the saints
mighty
To make round about me this night:

Drive from me every temptation and danger,
Surround me on the sea of unrighteousness,
And in the narrows, crooks and straits
Keep thou my coracle, keep it always.

Be thou a bright flame before me,
Be thou a guiding star above me,
Be thou a smooth path below me,
And be a kindly shepherd behind me,
Today, Tonight and for ever.

I am tired and I am a stranger,
Lead thou me to the land of angels;
For me it is time to go home
To the court of Christ, to the place of Heaven.

Traditional Gaelic

We have come a long way, Christianly speaking, from the justly criticised notion of 'submission to the will of God' which is in danger of weakening and softening the fine steel of the human will, brandished against all the powers of darkness and diminishment . . . I can only unite myself to the will of God (as endured passively) when all my strength is spent . . . Unless I do everything I can to advance or resist, I shall not find myself at the required point – I shall not submit to God as much as I might have done or as much as He wishes. If on the contrary, I persevere courageously, I shall rejoin God across evil, deeper down than evil; I shall draw close to Him.

Teilhard de Chardin

The poems printed below were written by a patient who spent seven months with us; she was almost blind and could not use her hands. She was adamant that she could not produce poems; however, after attending the workshop she eventually wrote several, dictating them.

'Off the Cuff' was composed only a few days before she died.

Starting Point

Where do we begin?
    At the starting point 'X'
And 'X' is also the unknown quantity
    Through 'X' we find 'Y'
'X' + 'Y' leaves us also questioning.
What are we questioning?
    What are we seeking?
I always seem to be looking for something –
    Even in dreams I am searching
For something – I am not sure what.
    Just as I seem to get there
Another door opens and the scene changes
    And I keep on walking and walking
Until the scene fades and I wake up
    The equation still unsolved.

Margaret Drake

Off the Cuff

Quite suddenly, off the cuff, it came to me,
'Midst our laughing, chattering, joking and repartee,
The cheery 'See yer!' 'Take care!' and 'Goodbyee!',
A sudden silence, slow unwinding,
blessed peace and solitude.

Margaret Drake

Thine eyes shall see the king in his beauty:
they shall behold the land that is very far off.

Isaiah 33.17

Nothing to Save

There is nothing to save, now all is lost,
but a tiny core of stillness in the heart
like the eye of a violet.

D. H. Lawrence

I rest on God, who will assuredly not allow me to find the meaning of life in his love and forgiveness, to be wholly dependent upon him for the gift of myself, and then destroy that meaning, revoke that gift. He who holds me in existence now, can and will hold me in it still, through and beyond the dissolution of my mortal frame. For this is the essence of love, to affirm the right of the beloved to exist. And what God affirms, nothing and no one can contradict.

John Austin Baker

Oh! think of stepping ashore,
And finding it heaven;
To clasp a hand outstretched,
And to find it God's hand!
To breathe new air
And find that celestial air;
To feel refreshed,
And find it immortality;
Oh! think to step from storm and stress
To one unbroken calm:
To awake and find it home.

Anon

In death we meet the conqueror of death; we meet love.

F. M. M. Comper

The Gate of the Year

I said to the man who stood at the Gate of the Year –
'Give me a light that I may tread safely into the unknown.'
And he replied:
'Go out into the darkness and put your hand into the hand of God. That shall be to you better than light and safer than a known way.'

Minnie Haskins

If I should die and leave you here awhile,
Be not like others – sore undone, who keep
    Long vigils by the silent dust and weep.

For my sake turn again to life and smile,
    Nerving thy heart and trembling hands to do
Something to comfort weaker hearts than thine.
    Complete those dear unfinished tasks of mine
And I perchance may therein comfort you.

Anon

I have seen death too often to believe in death.
    It is not an ending, but a withdrawal.
As one who finishes a long journey
    Stills the motor, turns off the lights,
Steps from his car
    And walks up the path to the home that awaits
him.

An American poet

5 *Resurrection*

Christian and Hopeful have come through the river of death:

Now upon the bank of the river, on the other side, they saw the two shining men again, who there waited for them. Wherefore being come out of the river, they saluted them, saying, We are ministering spirits, sent forth to minister for those that shall be heirs of salvation. Thus they went along towards the gate.

Now you must note, that the City stood upon a mighty hill; but the pilgrims went up that hill with ease, because they had these two men to lead them up by the arms: also they had left their mortal garments behind them in the river; for though they went in with them, they came out without them. They therefore went up here with much agility and speed, though the foundation upon which the City was framed was higher than the clouds; they therefore went up through the regions of the air, sweetly talking as they went, being comforted because they safely got over the river, and had such glorious companions to attend them.

The talk that they had with the shining ones was about the glory of the place; who told them that the beauty and glory of it was inexpressible. There, said they, is the Mount Sion, the heavenly Jerusalem, the innumerable company of angels, and the spirits of just men made perfect. You are going now, said they, to the paradise of God, wherein you shall see the tree of life, and eat of the never-fading fruits thereof: and when you come there you shall have white robes given you, and your walk and talk shall be every day with the King, even all the days of eternity. There you shall not see again such things as you saw when you were in the lower region upon the earth: to wit, sorrow, sickness, affliction and death; For the former things are passed away. The men then asked, What must we do in the holy place? To whom it was answered, You must there receive the comfort of all your toil, and have joy for all your sorrow; you must reap what you have sown, even the fruit of all your prayers, and tears, and sufferings for the King by the way. In that place you must wear crowns of gold, and enjoy the perpetual sight and visions of the Holy One; for there you shall see Him as He is. There also you shall serve him continually.

John Bunyan

In an ancient legend, Pilate's wife is said to be standing by the Cross on the afternoon of Good Friday. She turns to the centurion and says: 'Do you think Jesus is dead?'

'No, Lady, I don't,' is the answer.

'Then, where is He?'

'Let loose in all the world, Lady, where neither Roman nor Jew nor any other man can stop the victory of His Risen Life.'

Olive Wyon

There is a way of winning by losing, a way of victory in defeat which we are going to discover.

L. van der Post

How fair and lovely is the hope which the Lord gave to the dead when he lay down like them beside them. Rise up and come forth and sing praise to him who has raised you from destruction.

Syrian Liturgy

I climb a secret hill
Each Easter morn;
Not for to breathe my fill
Of wonder born
Anew on such a day;
But, more to hear
A trump immortal sound
Within mine ear,
A noise of viols
And a beat of drums,
Bugles that cry,
'He did not die
For aye;
Behold he comes,
Victor from death's
Red fray.'

Alistair Maclean

Christ it is that sustains you and calls you to dwell with Him. Laugh at the threats of disease, despise the blows of misfortune, care not for the dark grave, and go forth at Christ's summons, for Christ will be to each man a kingdom, a light, a life, a crown.

Edward Harman 1569
Burford Church

And he shall be as the light of the morning,
when the sun riseth, even a morning without clouds;
as the tender grass springing out of the earth
by clear shining after rain.

2 Samuel 23.4

As the moorland pool images the sun, so in our hours of self-giving thou shinest on us, and we mirror thee to men. But of the other land, our heaven to be, we have no picture at all. Only we know that thou art there. And Jesus the door and the welcome of each faithful one.

Alistair Maclean

Beloved, go and live thy life in the spirit of my dying,
in righteousness and love;
then truly shalt thou share my victory and taste my peace.

Hebridean Altars

Fresh Springs

That perfect balance
Between agony and joy
Given
Through His Cross and Resurrection.
The loving touch
Of His hands
Heals
Our wounded hearts and spirits
Making them whole.
His loving patience
With us,
His compassion for us
Blesses us
With fresh springs of love:
Unutterable joy.

Society of the Sacred Cross

Alfred the Great translates Boethius:

It is the eternal cry of the clay to the potter, 'Why hast Thou made me thus?' He will translate it, and after many days he will translate the answer, which is no answer in logic, but in excess of light.

'O Father, give the spirit power to climb
To the fountain of all light, and be purified.
Break through the mists of earth, the weight of
 the clod,
Shine forth in splendour, Thou that art calm
 weather,
And quiet resting place for faithful souls.
To see Thee is the end and the beginning,
Thou carriest us, and Thou dost go before,
Thou art the journey, and the journey's end.'

Translated by Helen Waddell

Deep Peace of the Running Wave to you
Deep Peace of the Flowing Air to you
Deep Peace of the Quiet Earth to you
Deep Peace of the Shining Stars to you
Deep Peace of the Son of Peace to you.

Gaelic traditional

References

1 THE SEARCH FOR MEANING

Thornborough, P., 'A Prayer', in *New Christian*, 2 April 1970.

Waddell, H.(tr.), *Lyrics from the Chinese*. London, Constable, 1943.

Waddell, H.(tr.), *Poetry In the Dark Ages*. (The eighth W. P. Ker Memorial Lecture, University of Glasgow, 1947.) London, Constable, 1958.

'Memorial Service for the Six Million', in *Forms of Prayer for Jewish Worship*. The Reform Synagogues of Great Britain, 1977.

Frankl, V., *Man's Search for Meaning*. London, Hodder & Stoughton, 1964.

Henke, E., a patient in St Christopher's Hospice.

Havelock Eyre, J., a patient in St Christopher's Hospice.

2 ANGER

Kushner, H. S., *When Bad Things Happen to Good People*. London, Pan Books, 1982.

'Zohar' and 'Chasidic' in *Forms of Prayer for Jewish Worship*. The Reform Synagogues of Great Britain, 1977.

Dominian, J., quoted in Priestland, G., *Priestland's Progress*. London, BBC Publications, 1981.

Clements, B., in *The Unity Book of Prayers*. London, Geoffrey Chapman, 1969.

Prescott, H. F. M., *The Man on A Donkey: A Chronicle*. New York, Macmillan, 1952.

Trimakas SJ, K. A.(tr.), *Prayers written by Lithuanian Prisoners in Northern Siberia*. New York, Paulist Press, 1960.

Pope John Paul II, reported in *The Times*, June 1982.

Baker, J. A., *Travels in Oudamovia*. Leighton Buzzard, Faith Press, 1976.

Lloyd, R., *The Borderland*. London, George Allen & Unwin, 1960.

Herbert, G., 'Love (III)' in *The Works of George Herbert*. Oxford University Press, 1941.

Priestland, G., *Priestland's Progress*. London, BBC Publications, 1981.

Maclean, A., in Reith, M., *God in Our Midst*. London, SPCK, 1975.

3 SUFFERING

Teilhard de Chardin, in Braybrooke, N.(ed.), *The Wind and the Rain*. London, Secker & Warburg, 1962.

Torrie, M., *Selected Poems*. Richmond, Cruse, 1979.

Levi Yitzchak of Berditchev, in *Forms of Prayer for Jewish Worship*. The Reform Synagogues of Great Britain, 1977.

Trimakas SJ, K. A.(tr.), *Prayers written by Lithuanian Prisoners in Northern Siberia*. New York, Paulist Press, 1960.

Appleton, G., *One Man's Prayers*. London, SPCK, 1967.

Baker, J. A., *Travels in Oudamovia*. Leighton Buzzard, Faith Press, 1976.

Sayers, D. L., 'The Just Vengeance', in *Four Sacred Plays*. London, Gollancz, 1948.

Baker, J. A., *The Foolishness of God*. London, Darton, Longman & Todd, 1970.

Catherine of Siena, in Wyon, O., *Consider Him: Three Meditations on the Passion Story*. London, SCM Press, 1956.

Warrick, G.(ed.), *Revelations of Divine Love*. London, Methuen, 1901.

Moule, H. C. G., *Christus Consolator*. London, SPCK, 1931.

Milner-White, E., *A Procession of Passion Prayers*. London, SPCK, 1956.

Taylor, J. V., original poem (unpublished), 1981.

Prescott, H. F. M., *The Man on a Donkey: A Chronicle*. New York, Macmillan, 1952.

4 DYING

Smith, S., *Selected Poems*. London, Longman, 1962.

Lawrence, D. H., *Selected Poems* (Viking Compass edition). New York, Viking Press, 1959.

Bunyan, J., *The Pilgrim's Progress*.

Clergyman's widow, in Blythe, R., *The View in Winter: Reflections on Old Age*. London, Allen Lane, 1979.

Goldin, G., 'Winter Rise', in *Poems of Aging*. Richmond, Patten Press, 1981.

An Isleman, in Reith, M., *God In Our Midst*. London, SPCK, 1975.

Reeman, S., a patient in St Christopher's Hospice, 1975.

Congreve, Fr., in Wyon, O., *Consider Him: Three Meditations on the Passion Story*. London, SCM Press, 1956.

Gelan, P., in *Forms of Prayer for Jewish Worship*. The Reform Synagogues of Great Britain, 1977.

Traditional Gaelic, in Reith, M., *God In Our Midst*. London, SPCK, 1975.

Teilhard de Chardin, *Le Milieu Divin*. London, Collins, 1957.

Drake, M., a patient in St Christopher's Hospice.

Baker, J. A., *The Foolishness of God*. London, Darton, Longman & Todd, 1970.

Comper, F. M. M., source unknown.

Haskins, M., source unknown.

5 RESURRECTION

Bunyan, J., *The Pilgrim's Progress*.

Wyon, O., *Consider Him: Three Meditations on the Passion Story*. London, SCM Press, 1956.

van der Post, L., *A Ban of Shadow*. London, Hogarth Press, 1954.

Syrian Liturgy, from Grail leaflets.

Maclean, A., in Reith, M., *God In Our Midst*. London, SPCK, 1975.

Harman, E., from a tablet in Burford Parish Church, 1569.

Hebridean Altars, in Reith, M., *God In Our Midst*. London, SPCK, 1975.

Society of the Sacred Cross, from a card (anonymous).

Waddell, H.(tr.), *Poetry in the Dark Ages*. (The eighth W. P. Ker Memorial Lecture, University of Glasgow, 1947.) London, Constable, 1958.